Too Much FUN Digging in the DIRT

Cheryl Robinson

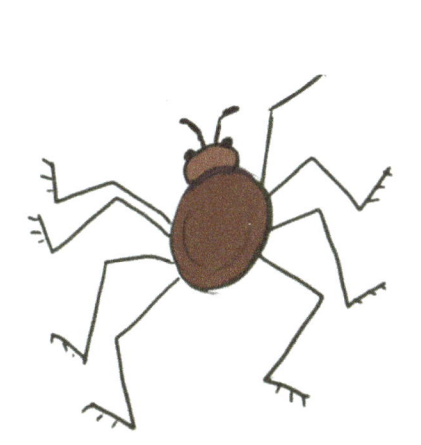

◆ FriesenPress

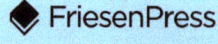

Suite 300 - 990 Fort St
Victoria, BC, V8V 3K2
Canada

www.friesenpress.com

Copyright © 2020 by Cheryl Robinson
First Edition — 2020

All rights reserved.

No part of this publication may be reproduced in any form, or by any means, electronic or mechanical, including photocopying, recording, or any information browsing, storage, or retrieval system, without permission in writing from FriesenPress.

ISBN
978-1-5255-6123-8 (Hardcover)
978-1-5255-6124-5 (Paperback)
978-1-5255-6125-2 (eBook)

1. *Juvenile Nonfiction, Animals, Insects, Spiders, Etc.*

Distributed to the trade by The Ingram Book Company

DEDICATION

Dedicated to all the grandmas, grandpas, moms, dads, and grandkids out there who love spending time together, and pass on their knowledge to another generation!

This book is especially dedicated to my own grandson, Tycen, who made my heart more stretchy with this exciting adventure!

One sunny day in the fall Gram and I ploughed through hard dirt in her garden

to make it really soft and velvety.

We pulled looooooooong roots of weeds with our magic mitted fingers.

Our fingernails stayed nice and clean.

We had **SO** much **FUN** that day!

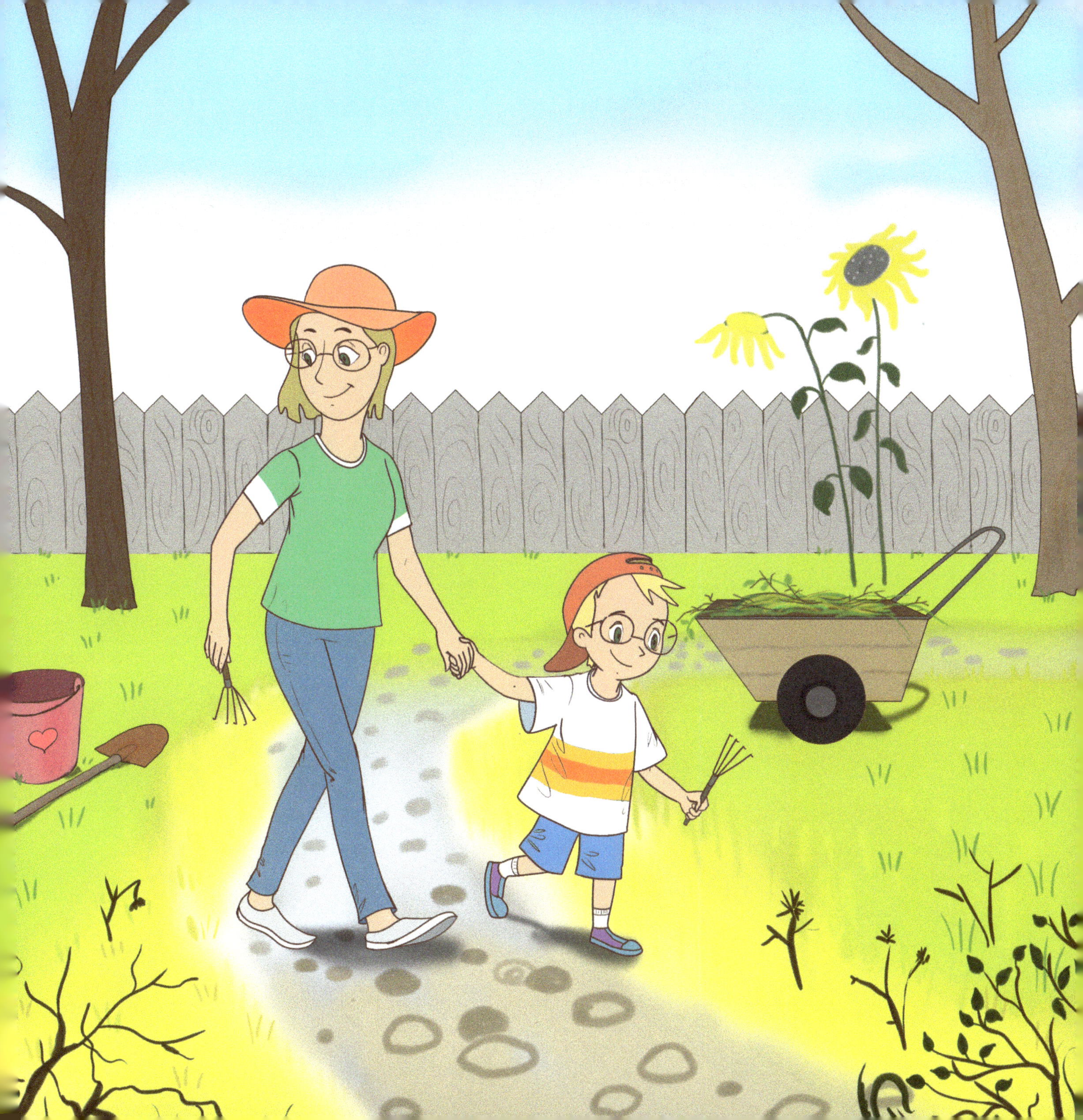

We saw insects and animals in the garden do some exciting things.

LISTEN...

I started to dig in the soil, and a big 'creepy-crawly' tried to climb right up on me just like I would climb a tree.

"EWW!"

I said, and shook it off.

Gram said these guys eat bugs, even mosquitoes!

She told me not to squish it because it was a majestic ...

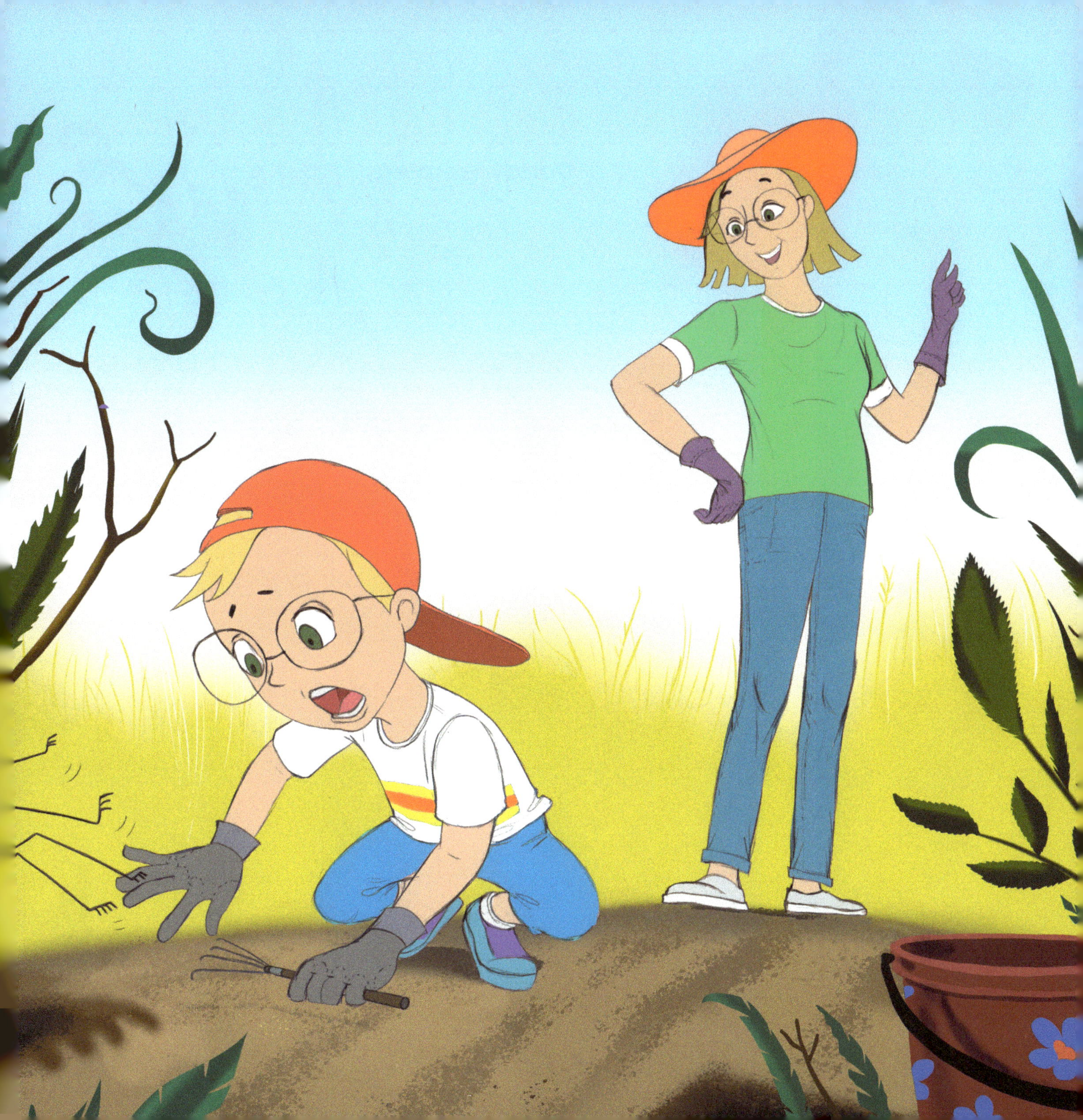

Daddy Longlegs!

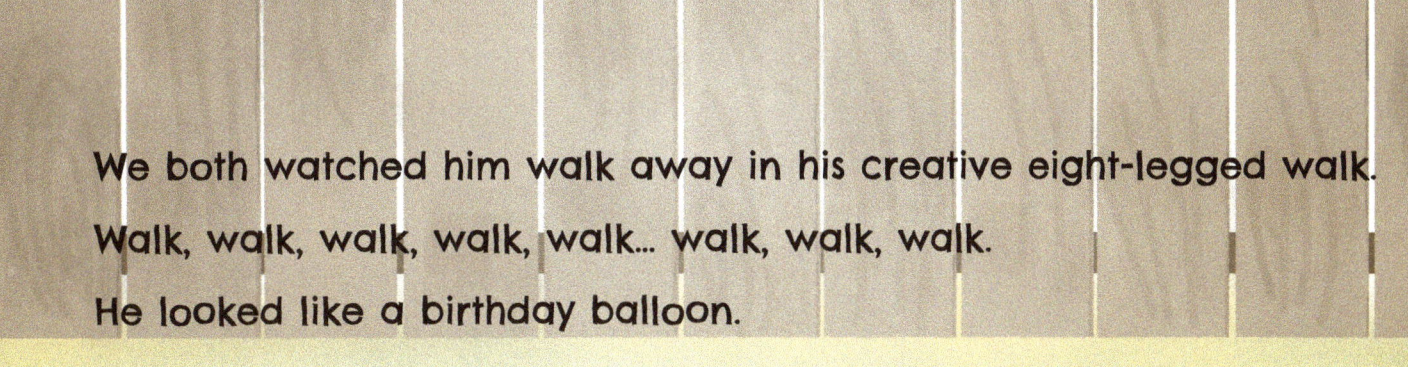

We both watched him walk away in his creative eight-legged walk.

Walk, walk, walk, walk, walk... walk, walk, walk.

He looked like a birthday balloon.

EIGHT LONG STRING-LIKE LEGS

were attached to his body.

We dug in the dirt and pulled more clingy roots from the flower garden. A pretty little red bug with black spots whizzed by.

She flew up from the soil so fast she could have been a homemade rocket!

She was a **LADYBUG**.
I know ladybugs are good. They eat stuff that's bad for plants.

Gram and I watched the ladybug and the spider dance away.

We think they got together for lunch that day.

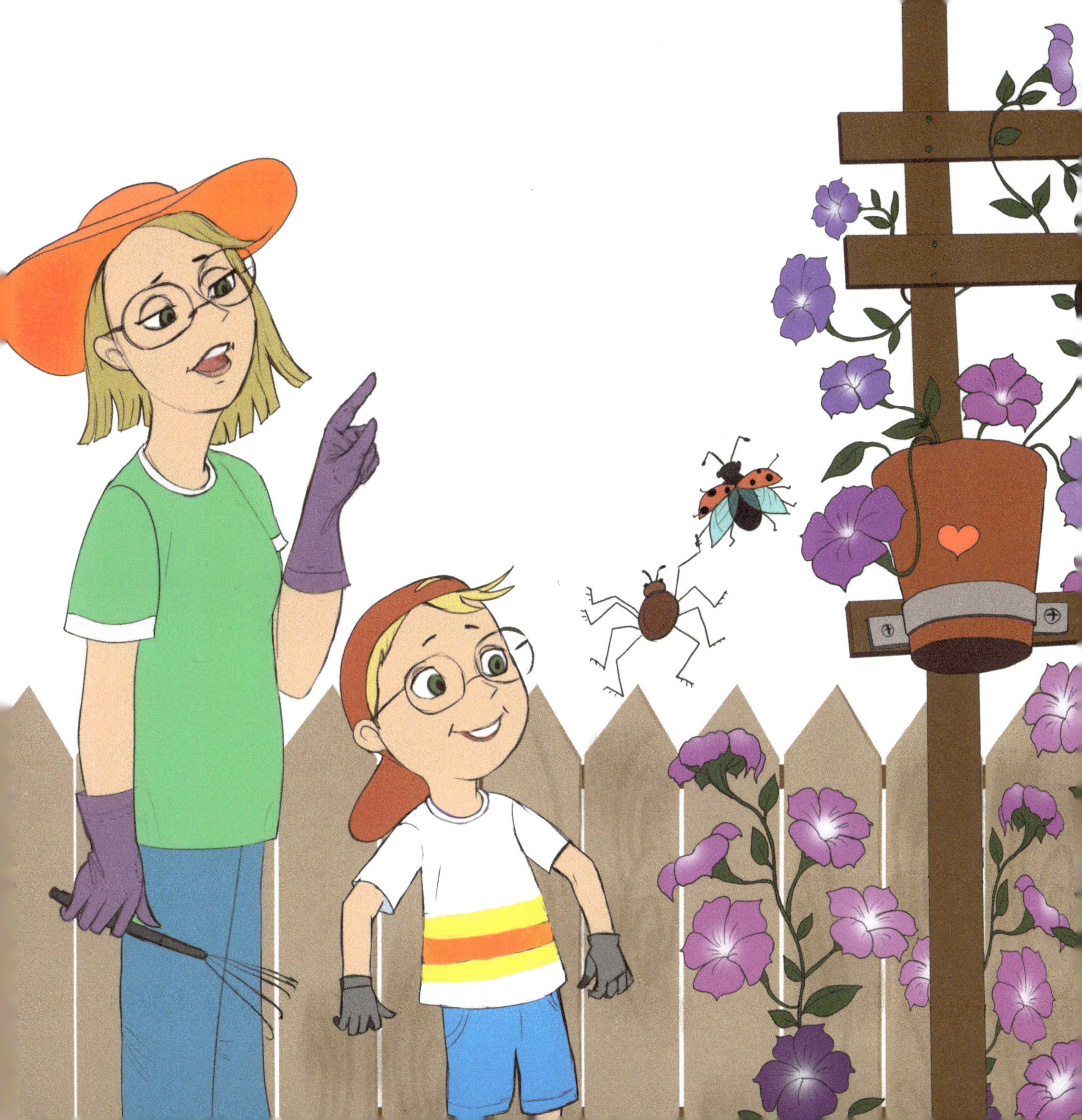

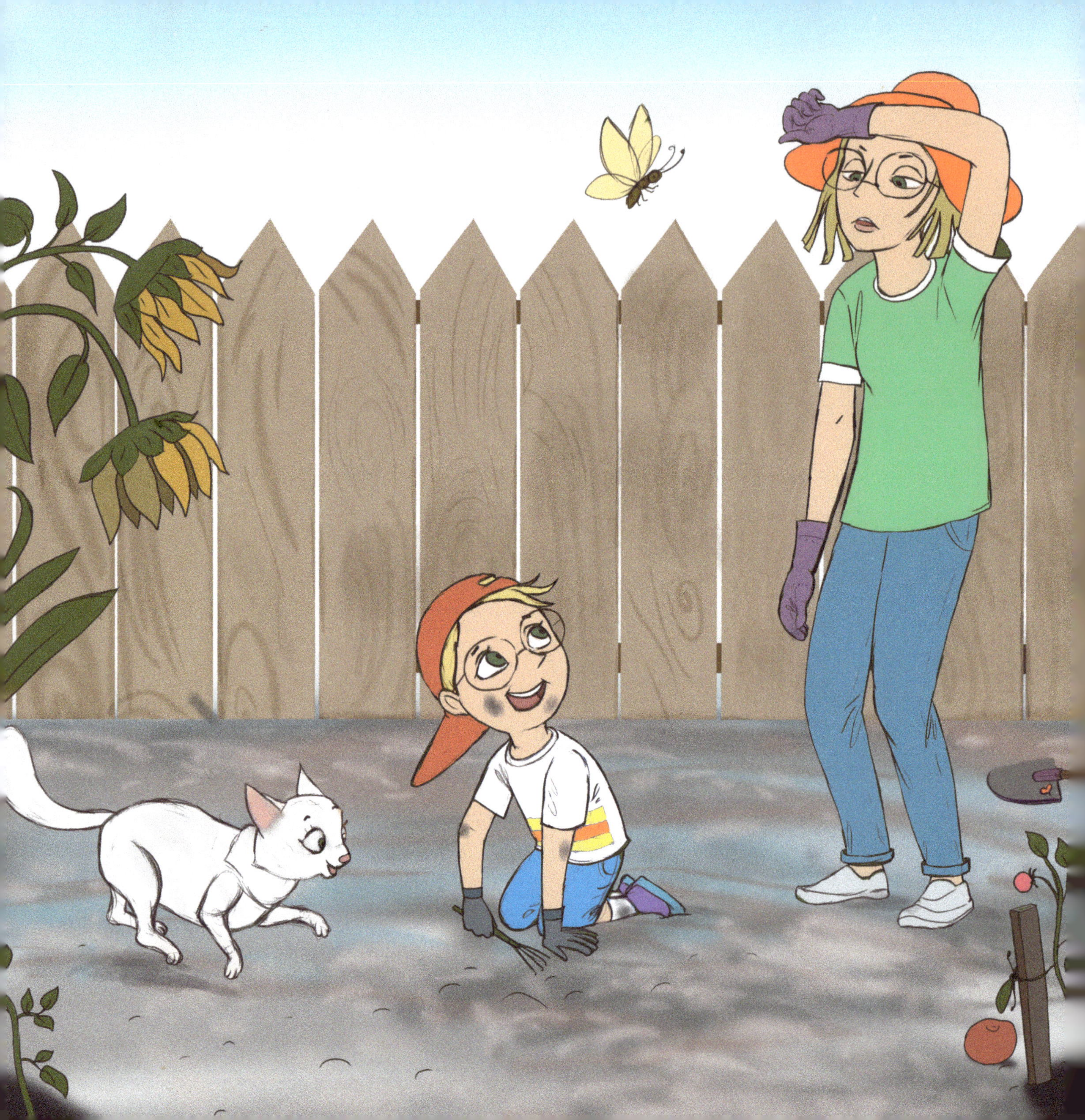

We were loosening the dirt when my fluffy white furball ran past.

I call him Sharp Tooth because he spits, **"PPPSSSTTT"**, and hisses, **"HHHSSSTT!"**

He even **BITES**. Gram doesn't like him when he does that. My kittycat's proper name is Snowbell.

He jumps a lot, and when he **JUMPS**, Gram and I think he's a Chicken Cat.

We think he acts like that because someone was mean to him when he was little.

Later, a big furry white dog with a "C" shaped tail came running through Gram's lawn.

The curious dog wagged his tail, and started CHASING Snowbell.

If only he had black stripes –

he could have been a **TIGER DOG!**
Snowbell ran away.

WHAT A CHICKEN CAT!

Gram and I growled a quiet tiger growl at the friendly dog –

"GRRRRRRRR!"

The tiger dog didn't even hear us. He ran back to his own family.

Snowbell climbed up into my treehouse, and LAUGHED at the run-away dog,

"Na, na, na, boo, boo!
You can't catch me, you chicken dog!"

I think Snowbell even STUCK OUT HIS TONGUE – my cat was trying to act tough.

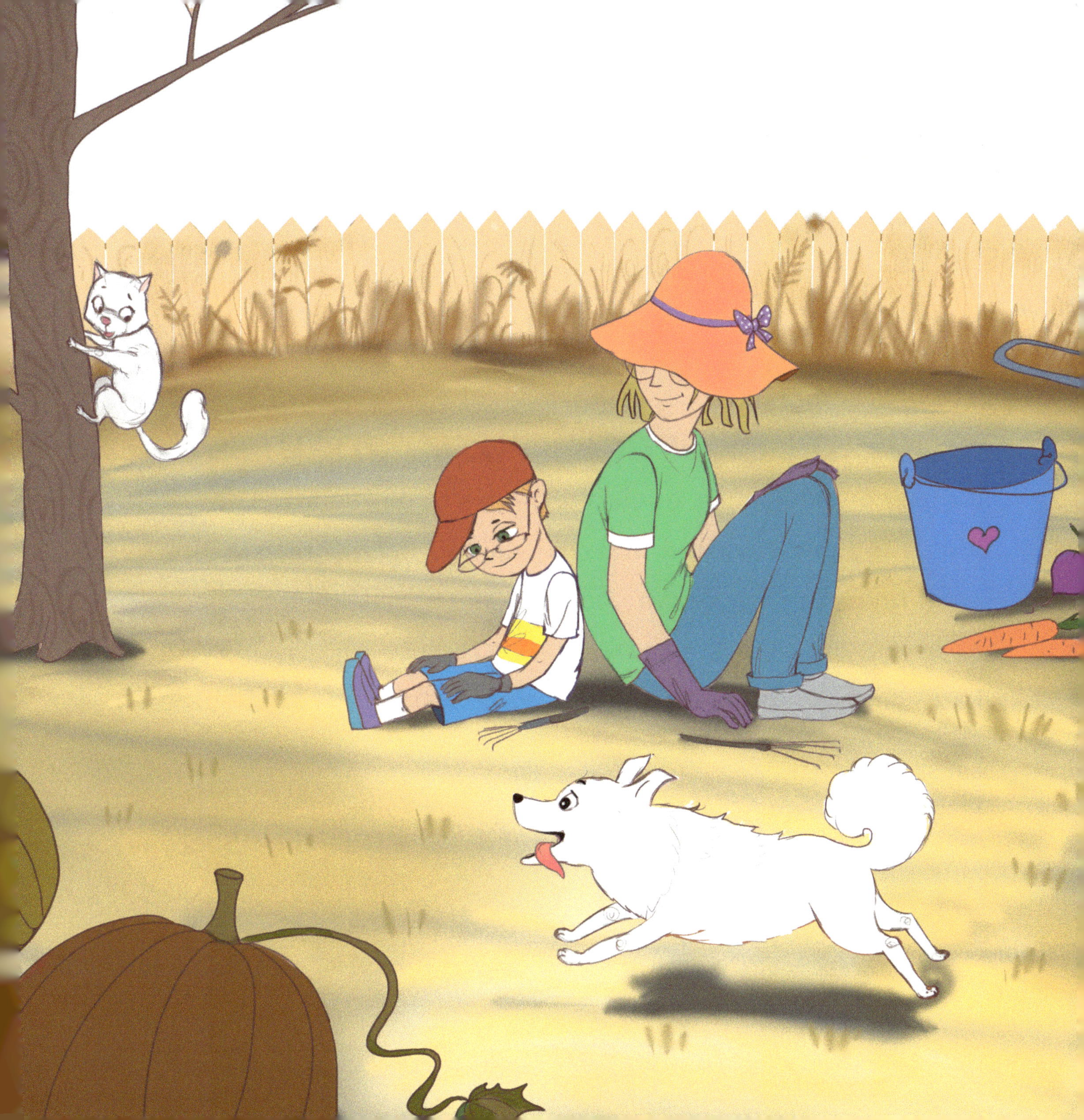

After a while, Gram's big grown-up cat ran up to Sharp Tooth on the lawn.

Snowbell jumped and flip-flopped in the air, as quick as a wink.

He startled us, and Gram said, "Snowbell is acting like a chicken cat again."

We flapped our elbows, and clucked,
"PUCK, PUCK, PUCK, PUCK, PUCK!"

But my beautiful white kitten didn't care at all.

Gram's big tabby cat ran away, so we flapped our elbows at him too.

Gram and I kept digging in the soil.

My eyes grew big when I saw a long creature with CENTIPEDE LEGS.

It wriggled out of the ground in the flowerbed and climbed up on Gram's mitts.

"EWW - DISGUSTING!"

Would you believe my grandma let that thing walk right back into the dirt?

Yes, she did let that thing walk right back into the dirt.

She said she would "research" to find out what that creature was.

Gram said some worms are good for the soil.

But I think some worms are NOT good for the soil.

That worm did not look good at all.

Gram doesn't kill many creatures.
Then I found what I thought was a CRICKET.

He had enormous GOOGLY eyes on each side of his head.
He was looking at me with a mad face – like a MONSTER!

Grandma grew up on a farm in Saskatchewan where big crusty bugs eat wheat and gardens.

She's heard them sound like a macaroni shaker
when they jump and fly, but not quite as noisy.

They even spit brown GUNK on your fingers.

"EWW! YUCK!"

Gram says her dad, my great grandpa, was a kid in the 1930'S, the time of THE GREAT DEPRESSION. He told her of a time when many grasshoppers ate the farmers' wheat in the fields, and when it was gone, some sneaked into his house
and ate the curtains!

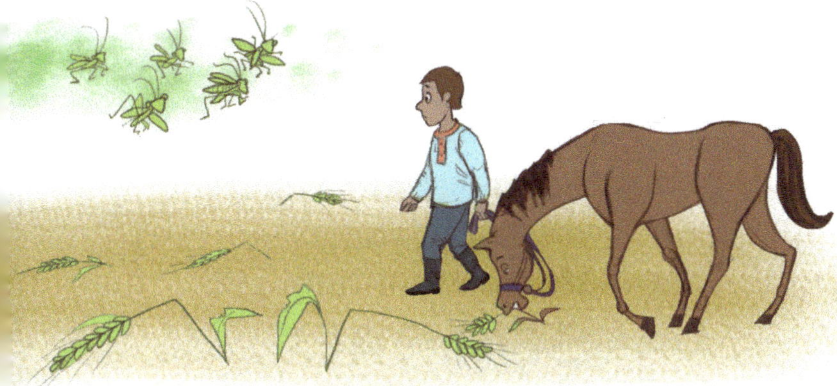

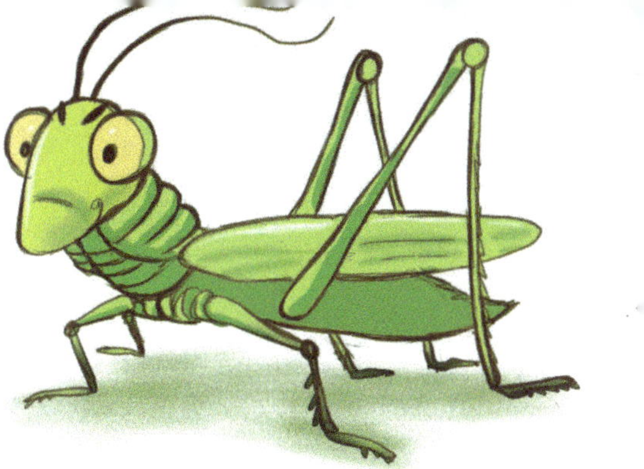

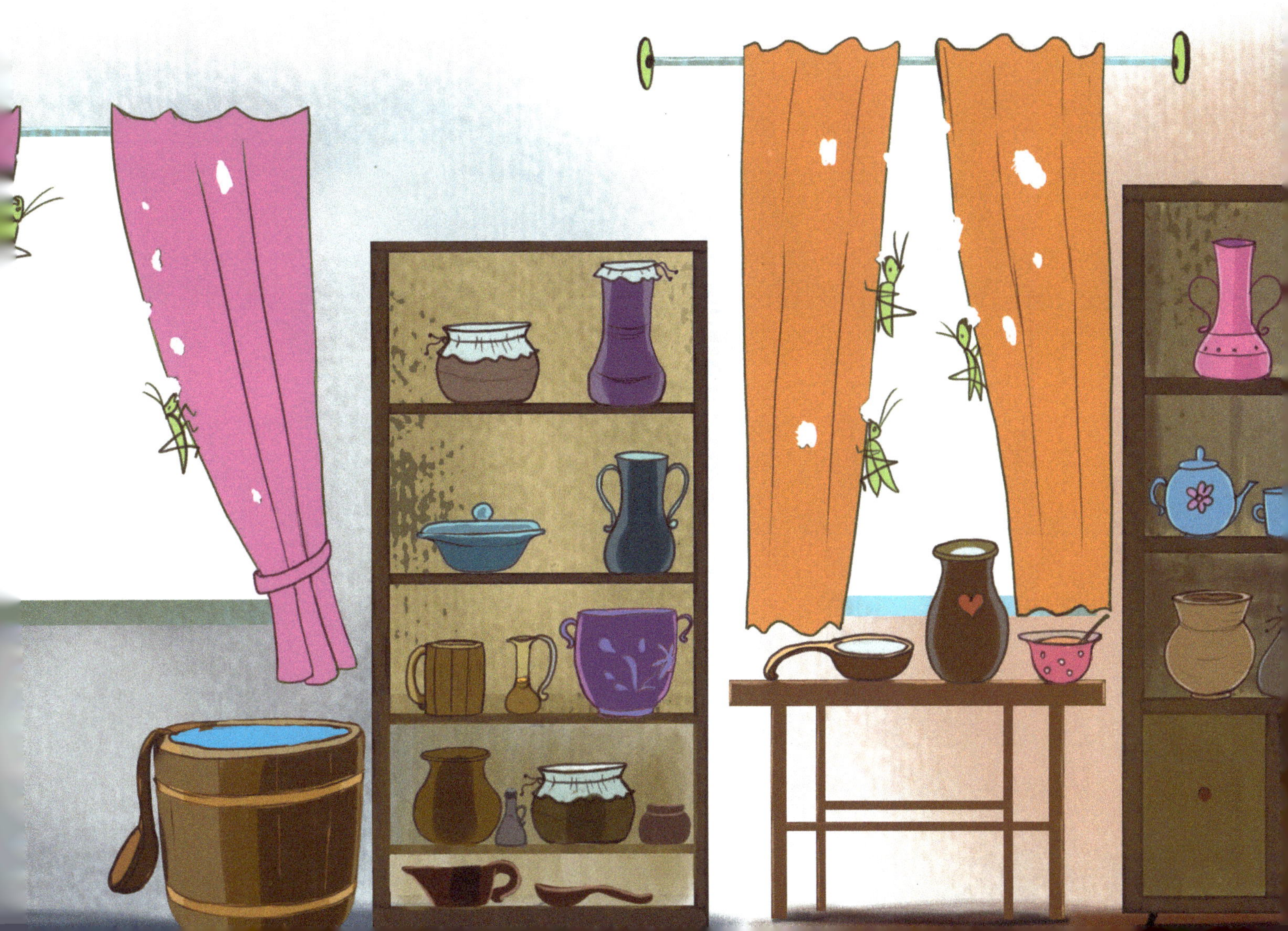

When I found that pointy-kneed wheat stealer, Gram stepped on him and **SQUISHED** him!

SHE SQUISHED HIM AS FLAT AS A PANCAKE!

Speaking of pancakes, we went inside for lunch.

Gram made grilled cheese sandwiches and soup with lots of wormy noodles.

We quenched our thirst with water, and thanked God for yummy worms and grilled cheese.

We needed good fuel after working hard in the sun.

After slurping up all the worms in my soup,
I had an Oreo cookie with milk for dessert.

UMM, UMM, GOOD!

Gram's cat kept staring at me. He wanted some milk, too.
I poured some of mine into his bowl, and we were all happy.

When God closes a door, He opens a window.

Afterwards, we went back outside, and some buzzy bugs started to bug us. Did our bright shirts attract them?

Or, Did they smell our chicken noodle soup?

YELLOW jacket wasps are so colourful –
THEY COULD BE CALLED THE FASHION BUGS!

Gram whispered that they probably wouldn't hurt us.
We didn't panic, but brushed them away–
and they didn't bite us.

We didn't see any long black, **BLUE** or **PURPLE** flying bugs.

We didn't see any **THIN ORANGE** ones or any round black and **YELLOW** striped ones.

These bugs love to hover like helicopters
and then fly away with their skinny wings.

Too bad – we spotted no dragonflies in flight.
Too bad – we spotted no butterflies or bumble bees in flight.

Oh, well, maybe next year when we work in the soil again!

We finished digging in the dirt.

We worked and sweated and got a LITTLE dirtier.

Gram is teaching me about her
CANADIAN HOPE...
that we should always dream big!

She says we can plant and grow special things in our hearts, too.
If something bad comes against us (like grasshoppers)
we will need courage and faith and hope!

It's fun to imagine what we CAN plant and grow...

Gram and I looked around at the dirt.

There were no weeds in our SUMMER-FALLOW (its farm name).
The soil in our garden was ready for a winter sleep.

Gram said land in the fall is kind of like a kid who needs a nap. God would help the land sleep in the winter so it could grow things well – next summer.

"Good night, soil.
GOOD NIGHT,
all you animals and bugs!"

Gram and I had enormous **SMILES** in our stomachs and on our faces! We smiled and felt good inside – kind of stretchy in **OUR HEARTS.**

Information sourced from the Net:

DADDY LONGLEGS are arachnids (not spiders) that have eight long skinny legs. These arachnids are very beneficial to a house or home. They are omnivores and eat insects, other spiders, pests like aphids, dead insects, fungus, bird droppings, worms, and snails.

LADYBUGS are not true bugs, but are beetles that are good for gardens. They don't eat plants, fabric, paper or any household items. They do like to eat APHIDS, and will often lay their eggs in aphid homes so their babies can quickly get aphid-food. Aphids are very small destructive pests that feed on plants.

EARTHWORMS are tube shaped creatures that eat leaves and grass. After eating, they "poop" out good fertilizer. They are like free farm help increasing the amount of air and water that gets into the earth. Earthworms can burrow into soil and create a drainage system. Not bad for a little worm, eh?

CENTIPEDES are good but ugly predators that feed on pests such as cockroaches, slugs, spiders, and flies. Their flat bodies have one pair of long legs per body segment. With at least 15 pairs of legs, they are not true insects. These arthropods can inject venom through pincers and inflict a painful bite.

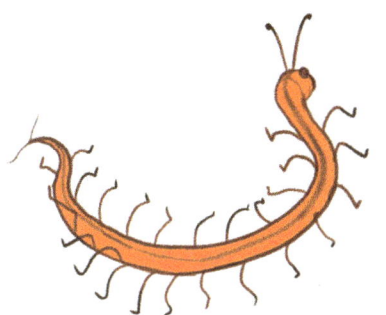

GRASSHOPPERS are ground dwelling insects with powerful hind legs which allow them to escape threats by leaping vigorously. They hatch from an egg into a nymph or "hopper" that undergoes five moults. As plant-eaters, a few species are serious pests of cereals, vegetables and pasture, especially when they swarm in their millions as locusts and destroy crops over wide areas, sometimes causing famine. They are used as food in countries such as Mexico and Indonesia.

CRICKETS are related to Grasshoppers! Their cylinder like bodies have round heads, long antennae, and leathery legs which rub together to 'chirp'. They are kept as pets or deep fried as snacks in different countries! Jiminy Cricket is famous in The Adventures of Pinocchio by Carlo Collodi.

YELLOW JACKET WASPS mostly feed on other insects like flies and bees. They also like picnic foods, fruits, dead bugs, and the nectar of flowers. Yellow jackets are attracted by sights and smells of flowers. They travel up to 1 mile from their nest which they are very protective of, and will attack if someone approaches within a few feet of that nest.
So, be careful!

BUTTERFLIES are insects which have the typical four-stage insect life cycle. Winged adults lay eggs that become caterpillars which feed on plants. Fully developed caterpillars pupate in a chrysalis. The skin splits, the adult insect climbs out, and after its wings have expanded and dried, it flies off as a butterfly. Metamorphosis is complete.

Most **BUMBLEBEES** are social insects that form colonies with a single queen bee. Their round bodies appear and feel fuzzy. Like honeybees, bumblebees feed on nectar, using long hairy tongues to lap up the liquid. Bumblebees feed pollen to their young. They use colour and spatial relationships to identify flowers to feed from. Bumblebees are important pollinators for agriculture.

Adult **DRAGONFLIES** are insects that have large, multifaceted eyes, two pairs of strong, transparent (see through) wings, and an elongated body. The wings of most dragonflies are held flat and away from the body. Dragonflies often have brilliant iridescent or metallic colours making them showy in flight. They are agile fliers.

ABOUT THE AUTHOR

CHERYL ROBINSON is a grandmother who loves spending time with her family. She did some waitressing, nursing, and bookkeeping after being a stay-at-home Mom for a decade, and for the last eight years -- ONLY by the grace of God -- she's instructed Aquacize and land Fitness classes for Older Adults. As things change in the middle of Covid-19, she keeps focusing on how full her glass is. A life-long learner, Cheryl continues taking courses, and enjoys Bible studies, thinking, reading, and writing. She's been married to her husband Dale for 43 years. They live in Nanton, Alberta, with their beautiful black and white cat, Prozac.

CPSIA information can be obtained
at www.ICGtesting.com
Printed in the USA
LVHW070534141220
674086LV00039B/1590